CONSPIRACIES
OF LOVE
AND DEATH

Bill McLaughlin

CONSPIRACIES
OF LOVE
AND DEATH

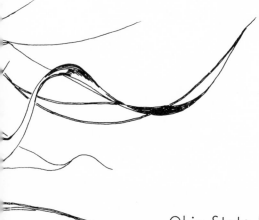

Ohio State University Press

Library of Congress Catalogue Card Number 72-102901
Standard Book Number 8142-0139-3
Manufactured in the United States of America

In memory of my parents & sister
who broke open poems
in their hands
and watched me gather them
until dark

CONTENTS

ACKNOWLEDGMENTS

The author wishes to express his gratitude for permission granted to include the following previously published poems in the present collection: "Sketches" 2 and 3, *Ambit*; "March," in "Songs," originally published under the title "March Song," *Foxfire*; "Sheep's Bone, Sheep's Hair," originally published in *liberal context*, Issue 12, Fall, 1964; "The Killers," the *Nation*, April 12, 1965; "Migrant Workers" and "Jazz Childhood," *Notre Dame English Journal*; "The Two of Us" and "Thief in the Garden," copyright 1965, and "Reply to a Storybook Question," copyright 1967, first appeared in *Quartet, a Magazine of the Arts*; and "Final Fruit," *Theo*.

Bill McLaughlin

CONSPIRACIES

OF LOVE

AND DEATH

1 | REPLY TO A
STORYBOOK QUESTION

No, not of horses. Not
of horses
was my childhood. Nor

of apple-strewn lawns
and lakes
and slapping fish-full

streams quickening with
silverish
fever through match-stick

swarms of young trees.
No, not of
these was my childhood,

but of neon-humid nights
stuffed with
bright calamities of the

eye; drunken heads of
women
cracked like eggs open

against the sidewalk; legs
sprawled in
false fracture, scrawled

obscenities in chalk
surrounding
like halos their heads

hung over the curb
into the
blinking wet midnight street.

And men with brown bottles
for thumbs
stuck securely at their mouths,

and the only horses were
giant-hoofed
defeated things struggling

with 2-ton trash bins, and
the only fish
were bug-eyed and smelled

of death; and streams were
huge corner
puddles from clotted sewers,

and the trees came not in swarms
but singly,
and stray dogs pissed on them.

Brown bodies stooped,
shirtless figures folded
in two— shimmering
under the sun throughout
the field like
scattered beads of coffee
on an earthen grille.

No movement; the air
hangs and simmers like a
dead weight, an invisible
congestion of heat pressing
the bent bodies in half
to the ground.

Suddenly, far out at the road
a lone speeding car
passes— almost soundlesly—
like the muffled intrusion
of a high-flying plane, and then
throughout the field
                    (first one,
then another)
                the daylight
silhouettes unbend,
                  (and another)
                      lift,
raise their wrapped straw-hooded
heads and, glancing silently,
seek out this noise, this
sound, this momentary reprieve . . .

Struck
dawn-still
in the prescience
of death,
the muscled
brownshimmering body
seeming a taut
immobile cast,
the head
      (root
of tangled tusks,
confusion of points)
cocked like the trigger
of its run,

it (crack!crack!crack!)
leaPed forward
Stag
gered
    jerked
to the ground like
the strings of a
puppet cut silently
one by one with invisible

bullets.

4 | NOVEMBER MOVEMENT

Water.
dropping like
insistent syllables
of an urgent
final message.

Trees.
poised glumly
wretched with the
weight of old
knotted breasts.

A road.
leading over
the hill where
clumps of brown
women listen while
the rain speaks.

5 | THE KILLERS

Through a rush of trees
I saw them come. Carrying
instruments of destruction across
their arms and shoulders
like precious steel icons
to be fondled for murder.

                                Intent,
and with the murmur of blood
about their eyes and mouths
they strode separately forward.
Five broad men in uniforms of death
kicking up dust as they came.

Then, abruptly, with resolute coincidence
those five slick steel sticks spat
angrily through the rush of trees
and somewhere past their leaden echo
a lone fractured pheasant
                                fell.

6 | THIEF IN THE GARDEN

I have labored long in search
of that stolen part of me
which disappeared some summers past
in that luxurious time when
last I called myself a child.

Now the very richness
of a rose garden eludes me,
and I can no longer lose myself
in the silent wealth of an autumn lake
or touch the mystery of Spring
when the last snow melts away.

But if I yearn for that stolen time
of innocence and sunburnt leaves,
I may only yearn —
and know myself as one of the thieves.

7 | SONGS

Dusk

birds invent space
spurn sleep
fill the gaping
hOle of light
                    with
collisions of air
Clutching swills of
quick darkness
in their drunken beaks.

Seasons

meanbastard Winter
stalks lateautumn fields
kicking last flowers to death

snow parachutes thickly to the
ground   Gargantuan silence
sheathes destruction

april umbrellas into Now
drenches earth with greengold music
exposing murder   until

May exquisitely nude arrives
flinging poems
into the mouth of death

Summer remains a forever rumor

Storm

Summer was declared today by
June
who fiercely flung her softly
hair
creating disturbances of
doom
as whip-lashed winds chastised
the air.

Sourcream-colored coin-sized
Moon
in hush balloon-struck tones
of bell
was about to threaten to rise at
Noon
when stars outblossomed & rained
like hell.

March

Cold
dripping
of cracked ice
and
wasted snow
melting
season into
season
as they go.

Soft
muttering
of saxophone
delight
and trumpet cries
as geese
flock sideways
down
sun-shot skies.

Touch
of sun
fingering
roofs
garden gates
penitentially
as wet-
mouthed
Spring waits.

Scorched flowers stand swollen
in sweet acrimony

Daylight flying-things collapse
and collide, dropping un-
bloodied to the ground

Birds, exhausted, bury smoked
feet beneath drooping breasts and
sit and study the burnt shimmer of their
shadows on the rocks below

While
everywhere the bald land flattens out
and cracks
in suppliance, offering
just a rising curse of steam
to the unceasing sun.

There were deepblue
mornings of stuttered
dawnbreaking
light
    (the moon a faded
bauble going blind in the
West)
    when, with a borrowed
frog's bass, I joined the crickets
in a cacophony of voiceless
delirium
      — a swelling of outrageous
delight.

Lend me the ears
of a child   and watch
how butterflies swarm
in breathless ribbons of
yellow
        to whisper
prophecies of a
farther time to me

Lend me the eyes
of a child   and see
how the muddy wings
of angels flutter from
trees and
            old autumn roads
at me, haunting an orange sky
with the wind

Lend me the mouth
of a child   and listen
while I weave soft litanies
of honey-locust leaves
to wind
            in the hair
of a youth searching for
nameless things

11 | EPIPHANY

When— in the latesummer
emptysouled Montreal—
I penniless trudged all hot
and starving across
town in search of a friend
of a friend who
might loan the poet pennies
for food and such

suddenly from across
a burntgreen city park
came an adolescent
all in foul beauty, with
a small soiled brother
curled and sleeping
in his arms

came an apparition
of innocence, all huddled
and sour, to frighten
the pity from my soul
and leave me wounded and
watching with wonder
the bent flapping sole
of my shoe—
so all in foul beauty they came.

12 | SAY FINIS

Friendships
failing
          falling
slow
     -motion
thru the years

clattering
mutely
          scatter-
ing
     like dead
butterflies

tossed with
grace
          -less
rhythm
          down
a deep dark well.

(1)

I dreamt (last
night
) an ocean
of ironrusted
fish

of tarsmooth (
inkdrop)
sharks with
fins quite tickle
-ish

May he rust in
peace
they said in
finest fishfoul
breath—

O funny funny fish
were
they who
tickled me to
death.

(2)

O God created the world
they say
in just one restless week

land and sky and water
one day
and next striped tiger sleek

plus four more days for
conjuring
the fawn and infant lamb

and then last day with slime
of earth
picked up & fashioned man.

(3)

Red and
yellow and
orange balloons
cascade
to the cartwheel
sea

    bumpingly
bobbing like
slowmotion rocks
heaved down
by some sand-dune
genie:

    bright
stickless
taffies, each
deliciously
skips

    over curled
licking
seatongues
foamed white at
the tips:

       finally
harsh seabreath
with stern stormful
eye

     scatters
them into
a polkadot
sky.

| MISSING THE POINT

people make love too much
in a hurry

with counterfeit ungently
passion —

while outside the wind with
narrow eyes

sips serenely rain from
flowers' mouths —

and night unsuddenly moves
the moon

through a thousand hipsmooth
smiles.

15 | FINAL FRUIT

Grow me a tree of fruit
and I promise you, love,
I shall climb it
clutching the fruit as I go
shoving it hungrily
into my mouth,
swallowing even the seeds
as I climb to your warm body
waiting like a final
full roundness at the top.

Under the cold cast of the moon
we will exchange
the seeds of our bodies
and grow ripe
by the time of the sun.

1955/ONLY YOU

I don't own anythingany
more
except the sneaks I wore
the summer I was twelve
& rolling in the dark wet grass
with her

She was fifteen & taught me
to want to climb into her body
& out the other side

Her father forbid her
to see me
because I was Catholic
& so we met at night in the wet
grass behind dark houses

    hearing only
    the splash of our mouths above
    the drone of crickets

    seeing only the giant
    contours of eyes & nose we pressed
    against each other

feeling nothing
but the stones & twigs & dead
apples under our new bodies

lying beneath stars
& the stark spires of trees
our flesh hard & soft & soaked

gasping
slapping together
like wild fish at the bottom
of a blueblack sea

Our favorite song was
Only You by the Platters
& she even bought me the record

I smashed it a year later
when I heard she screwed a sailor
and had a baby

I don't own anythingany
more
except the sneaks I wore
& my wife always tells me that she
belongs to me

CELEBRATIONS

(1)

we were trees then
deep dark bark & sweet
growing entangled together

knuckles of yearning
scraping the sky

the moon a silver mouth
blowing perfect smokerings
through our hair

owls like sullen children
nesting at our wrists

crows astride my cock
frantic black flapping
into a white sun

the smell of rain
heavy as wet morning willows
by afternoon
we carved our bodies into dust

shook dandelion fists at the sky

(2)

all night
we drank wine with our hands
offered bread
with our eyes stuffed with candles

until blood

squeaked in my jaw like dry
white muscle
and I mined giant diamonds

down the dark of your throat

MEDITATION
ON THE CRUCIFIXION

(I)

Arms like tangled lengths
of thick spent cord
stretch
upward and away
as though frozen into pain
and twisted legs collapse
at the knees
pretending to catch the weight
of this outreach

Whose nails are these stuck
like fierce markings
of indication
in this bone-stabbed flesh?
And whose force dared drive them through?

(II)

Crowned head, torn weight
of head topped with sweet flowered spikes
from some dank Spring field, carried
like awful candles to your birthday head

and sunk unlit through your skull.
Sunk without burning to your God's brain

Whose coarse hands snatched
cold March thorns
to wind their sharp ring about your head?
And who stabbed you with this crown?
Who brought this wooden crown?

(III)

Warm unclotted God's blood
runs red with water out your open side,
beating gaudy streaks of death
down staggered ribs—those shrinking
glistening prongs of bone—lacing
ugly ribbons of sweat past your stomach
past your groin and down two crashing legs
infinitely steeped in retribution.

Whose steel lance carved
the sacred meat of your chest open
like some aboriginal tabernacle
of ultimate sacrament?
Yes, whose blade broke it open unto us?

ASH WEDNESDAY

Christians proclaiming
their worth
with a handful of dirt

smudged inscrutably
across
their scrubbed foreheads;

scents of soap and ash
struggle
for predominance above

the hundred pairs of
downcast
piously pouting eyes.

Resolutions rehearsed
silently—
Lenten oaths against

the devil of the flesh;
remembrance
of the coming Passion

and Death clouds the
mind,
fogs the fervent brain.

Thus insulated they spill
from church
into waiting cabs & buses,

wipe their weighted brows
and rush
confidently back to life.

ANTITHESES: PETITION
FOR THE DEATH OF A GOD

Christ
God, consubstantial
spectre of bloodied wine
and torn flesh, tortured
Son of the impotent Father of angels
and men whose love was empty
and so twice failed;

Christ
God, violent Lamb of
retribution whose example
stuffed rags in the
mouths and brains of mindless
caesars and totalitarian
saints of Jehovah;

Christ
Lord, outlaw lover of
the possessed, the poor,
the ignorant, the oppressed
and confused: poet & startled protector
of the sinner: gypsy
brother of the disinherited;

Christ
God, who would recreate
the world in your own Image, away
from the incalculable
crimes of your Father's conspiracy
against Love: You who suffer still
the spiked suicide of Redemption;

(Christ: Lord)
You who were the supreme
tragic hero before all time and forever:
Whose face is the face
of the clown's terror: of the lover's
countless secret hurts: of the fool's
impossible tenderness

   Hear us, now
at the hour, in the night of our dread:
   Come again
with rags to stuff full the vessels of violence:
   And deliver
us: Christ: Lord: God: Our Fool: from ourselves
   and the imperatives of evil.

SHEEP'S BONE, SHEEP'S HAIR

. . . *And after this our exile*
Show unto us the blessed fruit
Of our misery,
The rewards that Gods devise
To repair such misery
As is stretched across the span of lives,
Stretched and pulled bitterly
Up about the mouths and eyes
Of our dislocated days,
Our long enduring days
Lived to the quick and full moment of our cries:

Let them come unto Thee.
  We have suffered
    And would suffer Thee.

Out of the broken measure of our lives,
Out of the wide rack of our suffering
Drawn tight about our prayers,
Out of the dark hope we keep
For release from the snares
Of Satan and our Flesh,
Out of the dim promise we share
With the heedless rush

Of men across the boundary of years—
The promise of an eternal wedding
Of God and man, the joining
Of Sheep's bone with sheep's hair. . .

From out of all this Grant us peace and a sleep,
And if nothing more, a forgetting. . .

PORTRAITS AT THE
UNEMPLOYMENT OFFICE

(1)

Annimae (eighteen and
jussup from Sow Cahlina)
suddenly come roarin
(hair fluFFed crowfeathers)
thru the door,
                    bobs & weaves
Up to the counter
                    (planet eyes sunk
in midnight   mouth widens
to a disordered galaxy of tE-tH)
shuffles her slacksheathed legs (myG
-od!those uncontrollablyRolling hips!)

                    And (breasts
lolling lugubrious, sad balloons) says
                                    Hey
sugah who got Annimae's check
                              — huh?
                    Turns
struts hipsgiggling thru the door
                    ,unnotionably Obscene.

(2)

Her mouth (Barbara
Jean's) loops around (Barbara Jean's lazy

lips spread) like a
DRoopiNG clothesline of
(stringthin quivering)

crimson moistness.
Above her eyes (right
overtop like mis-

placed bruises) loom
thick mascara storm clouds
rumbling silently

while overhead (still
higher, zooming askance)
pencilled colliding

brows (one wider
more angled than the other)
stretch sharply

(puncturing infinities
of air) off either side of the
splattered canvasface.

(3)

Vincetta

your eyes
scoops
of blackened burning midday suns

face
the shape and shimmer of seawet
morning gulls

delicate stab of your neck speaks
a thousand
swans' deaths

(4)

Sweet black Edna, your body
is sweet, Edna, black
and pure as a caress of deep
midnight, Edna
                    your body
moves in a parade of ungloomed
shadows, mysterious & sweet,
black Edna, as the scent
                    of wet
Spring leaves which inherits
your hair, sweet Edna, black
and rolling and soft as
latesummer storm clouds
                         gathering
for rain.
            Only sweeter.

Black bar mid nig
ht mur
    mur of moth
-a
fucker shouts Boo
galoo
   Gal
      oo
   g
a loo
      into
sweet
six tin
trumpet ears

&

suddenly dead Otis
sing
Try
    a little ten
  der
       ness

I came to you
haltingly,
bearing the untried
blossom of my love
in arms weaker
than I supposed,
in arms no stronger
than your own

and you watched me come

I came to you
feeling my way
as through a
daylight dream of
thick fascination,
flowers falling
falling with the unsure
rhythm of my feet

and you watched me come

I came to you
spoiling my gift
as I came,
losing and letting fall
the frail burden
of my approach
as a child loses water
from some precious pail

and you let me pass by

25 | FARE ENOUGH

Give me tokens of your love
and I'll buy

all-night rides to the moon
in a desolate

melon-green trolley-car.
Clanging madly

on the bell, I'll scatter
strings of stars

sparking under the whining
steel wheels

and the sour-fruit moon
will grow

bright with my coming.

Loud with the absolute silence
of quiet understanding
we sit, the two of us,
like starved dumb servants
at some glorious feast —
twin invalids, each afraid
the other might dare to creep,
afraid we might race together
down some loud sequestered landscape
of irreverent joy;
                    and so
like sad and painted clowns
we remain — with polished smiles
of persistent regret, bashful fruit
on some golden bough.

27 ADULTERY

What is this burning
this nameless consummation
that flickers and dies
in the deep of my groin?

My torch wanes and falls
like an old candle
gone the way of its wax
after some conflagration

and somewhere I feel
an odd emptiness stir & grow
into a small satiety
of fragrant ashes

sweetening the silence
of our sleep
after the smoke
after the unholy fire.

the women of the world
passed me by last night
and not one of them chose
to observe
       the wild green stares
I placed at their feet
            and which
ran unintended up their tall
fleshy trunks, settling
at long last in the drooping
gray hollow of their eyes
       their eyes
the drooping gray hollow

       their eyes

A circus is Love and we
like lions tread
carefully sawdust-cushioned
cage;
      under tented imitation
of sky, low-throated teeth-strained
growls are exchanged;
                turning
clawfully to opposite corners
we sit wide-mouthed, deliciously
eschewing each other.

As I lay sleeping
heavy in your lap
beyond the endurance
of a more savage soul

I dream of your waist as
heavy at my loosened belt
and the warm rush
of your breath & fingers

soothing & tempting
my mouth   my words
my entire body

pretending sleep
I watch you as from
far below

watch the slow sound
of your lashes moving
heavily   heavily

watch the quick spread
of your mouth across
the pale flower of your face

feel the full-breathed
beat of your heart
against the shell of my ear

sounding like old oceans
out of my childhood
through the swell of your breast.

We thought we knew
             our bodies,
thought we knew their separate stories
like private tales whispered
             in a solitude
      of lust,
privately told, privately delighted, pri-
                   vately rehearsed
      for the double telling.

Why, then, so anxiously
             so full of music
did I listen as you played
      upon that instrument
I thought I knew, stringing
new songs and melodies
      from it   as though
from a different source
      a different instrument
altogether?

32 | SECRETS

*no one knew that you tormented/ a hummingbird
of love between your teeth . . . —-F. Garcia Lorca*

Nor, beloved, did they know
that you suffered
the fierce burning of almonds
sunk like eyes below
your forehead in magnolia-
scented scoops

nor could they have guessed
at the pale green lightness of the moon
slung like a buckle of fruit
at your waist

nor of your thighs thrust
like incredible candles of narrowing
white wax in the blistering
blood-shot sand.

(1)

Janet at just
sixteen
is impossibly
built
for brief stares

her body in-
vites
to be climbed
slowly
as one dares
:
bloomingly
knee-deep with
surf
awash her thighs

covetous wave
attacks
her breasts
drowns
a thousand eyes

(2)

(black cats at the corner
hung

white chick swings past,
young)

       - girl's a natural
                 fox
                 man

        - a stone clean bitch
                      for
                      sure

(they dig her rumbling
buttocks

in absolute rap-
port)

(3)

the old man sits
in his coat and hat
with his back to the wall
in the summer heat

    whiskey gums rehearsing
    rhymes
    silent eyes as thin as
    dimes

in his coat and hat
with his back to the wall

    socks sucked into balding
    shoes
    evabody gotta pay some
    dues

the old man sits
in the summer heat

    counting passing nylon
    legs
    Lawd have mercy on a man who
    begs

with his back to the wall
in his coat and hat

    tapping flapping toes in
    time
    clinging to his whiskey
    rhyme

in the summer heat

    one old monkey don't stop no
    show
    let them howlin four winds
    blow

the old man sits
in his coat and hat
with his back to the wall
as cool as hell.

(SPICS)N(SPADES)

Cat called Mr Clean come
into Shorty's this night (me
the soul gray boy in the bar)

heavy dude, you
know
       black bald head wrapped
in a woman's red wig

              strut soft down
one side the horseshoe bar
   fingerpoppin
              diggin hisself
        , you know

    hesitate at the curve
give a deep nod to the brothers
                    in the band

        pull
     on his goatee a little you know,,
         then

            diggin
     all the sisters groovin
with Spanish cats

        he glide
on ice past them all to a stool

& burn all 23 (you know) before his scotch chaser

Whose preternatural jester, you?
What rash surreal Lorca-dream spawned
your rainbow-stuttered face, that hyperbolic
ashcan face of gray death?

What cosmetic witch stroked
wild brows across the tops of your
eggshell drooping eyes?
And who dared draw careless lines
of thick wondering
through your wrinkled front clown's skull?

Those ears, those airplane ears crashing
sideways down your caved-in head,
small dumb cups of hearing, who brought
them bleeding from a donkey's grave?

Beneath an orange painted smile
spreads your natural line of gloom,
a thin quickening of hurtful lips
kissing the chin with some clown's secret
as your eyes melt to meet with mine.

In the morning
from formal
dehyde the general
plucks
a gleaming wreath
of bullets
inserting
them for teeth

gargling he
clears
the bloody phlegm
from
righteous lung
to throat
to bayon
eting tongue

without pause
he sets
his holstered mine
to the care
& combing
of his
electrified
barbed hair

over breakfast
coffee & guns
while quoting
bits
of martial law
he burps ex
ploding chil
dren out
his bomb-bay jaw

| STILL LIFE

Life
is a photo-
graph forever
to be taken
(said somebody or other)

mean
(-while poorsport old)
God finger-
taps nervously
at the shutter.

38

THE WAR—HEARD FROM
THE BEACH AT ATLANTIC CITY

Thousands of somewhere miles beyond
    miles beyond somewhere this oceansounding twilight shore
      of scattered darkdiving delicate gulls
somewhere a thousand skies goneby
        this searoar fragilefalling summer night
          & into glistening junglesteamed morning

        there is the earthshuddering shriek & BOOM of death
    of brainless widemouthed deepthroated darkeyed cannon
breathlessly stuttering young lives
          into the morning mud

          where by bloodmoist sunfall
    the wind comes sadly with delicate fingers
  to rustle vainly some silent standing flowers
as though magic bells of waking flagging forlorn aside
            the mudcased downfaced heads

    And the wind enraged swells suddenly wild
and blows the flowered stench of death
      across a thousand skies of sea to me.

is
a dry mouth
with blistered lips
and a blind
roofless throat

is
a collapse of
rough bloodless gums
gorging a
flower's moist lips

is
a breath of
foul ash brimming
a dumb
cavernous mouth.

It was
early May and the dogwoods
were just ending
their bloom; wilted
pinks and whites rung
the driveway
like a sorry wreath;
outside her windows some
dull birds
twittered monotonously
against a smoked sky

and she was dead:

her hydrocephalic head
m o t i o n l e s s
as a doll's on the pillow
and the blind
brown eyes half-shut
as though
for once its twisting
painful weight had somehow
slipped her damaged mind
and she lay lost
in a reverie of incredible
comfort

but she was dead:

the lower lip brutally
discolored,
a red and violet bruise
where her teeth
in final convulsion
must have bitten down
savagely
in breathless pain or
release

for she was dead:

was dead

dead

41 | WARREN J. McLAUGHLIN
(1912-1967)

I met my father just when he
died: with a wet kiss
on his gray whiskered
cheek we met: sitting softly
through the long idle
silence of the wide
white room: we met among
his last fitful dreams, between
the shared delirium
of memory's neglected love:

just 24 years together when
we finally met: during
visiting hours we came
together: lost childhoods
at last gone, hands clasped
bony and smooth, eyes dry with
a deeper crying, we met
and exchanged ourselves when
he   just   died.

why not dwell in worlds of If
where messengers of Wish prevail
unbounded by Actually's cliff
escaped from Impossible's dark jail?

we'd live in golden cloud-thatched huts
encircled by bright crashing streams
and look across to where grim Buts
set out with Musts to murder dreams.

43 | POEM

Since you never knew I was lost
will you remember
to come find me? Scrape me together
out of old rags, sweep
my dust from under steeples
and wooden horses?

Study my calendar of poems,
sing me back
from the black silence of balconies,
search the handlebars
of bikes?

Invent caves? Discover me among
green graves of children,
rake me open in black fields, till me
spill me over
into the fertile flesh of you?

  you will find me among
  friends,
  dying of strangers